THIS BOOK BELONGS TO

_____

FOR THE KIDS WHO WANT TO BE A SECRET NINJ

ISBN: 9798894582344

IN A QUIET VILLAGE, YOUNG KAI TRAINED TO BECOME A GREAT NINJA.
HIS DREAM WAS TO GO ON A MISSION LIKE THE OLDER NINJAS.

ONE SUNNY MORNING, SENSEI MEI GATHERED THE NINJA STUDENTS.
"KAI," SHE SAID, "TODAY, YOU'LL GO ON YOUR FIRST MISSION!"

KAI'S HEART RACED WITH EXCITEMENT. "WHAT'S THE MISSION?" HE ASKED.
"YOU MUST RETRIEVE THE GOLDEN CHERRY BLOSSOM FROM THE
FORBIDDEN FOREST," SAID SENSEI MEI.

KAI BOWED DEEPLY. "I WON'T LET YOU DOWN, SENSEI!"
SENSEI MEI SMILED. "REMEMBER: PATIENCE, FOCUS, AND KINDNESS ARE A NINJA'S
GREATEST TOOLS."

KAI PACKED HIS SMALL BAG WITH NINJA STARS, A ROPE, AND WATER. "GOLDEN CHERRY BLOSSOM, HERE I COME!" HE WHISPERED, SETTING OFF.

THE FORBIDDEN FOREST WAS DARK AND FULL OF STRANGE SOUNDS.
KAI TOOK A DEEP BREATH. "STAY CALM, LIKE SENSEI MEI SAID," HE
REMINDED HIMSELF.

AS KAI WALKED DEEPER, HE HEARD A RUSTLE.
"WHO'S THERE?" HE ASKED, GRIPPING HIS ROPE TIGHTLY.

A TINY RABBIT HOPPED OUT OF THE BUSHES, TREMBLING.
"OH NO! ARE YOU STUCK?" KAI GENTLY FREED THE RABBIT FROM A THORNY
VINE.

THE RABBIT TWITCHED ITS NOSE.
"THANK YOU!" IT SQUEAKED.
KAI LAUGHED. "YOU'RE WELCOME, LITTLE FRIEND."

THE RABBIT JUMPED UP. "IF YOU NEED HELP IN THE FOREST, CALL ME!"
THEN IT DASHED OFF INTO THE TREES.

KAI SMILED AND CONTINUED WALKING. SUDDENLY, HE CAME TO A WIDE RIVER.
"HOW WILL I GET ACROSS?" HE WONDERED.

KAI NOTICED A FALLEN TREE STRETCHING ACROSS THE RIVER.
"I'LL BALANCE LIKE A NINJA!" HE SAID, STEPPING CAREFULLY.

HALFWAY ACROSS, A STRONG WIND BLEW!
KAI WOBBLED, BUT HE STAYED CALM. "FOCUS, KAI," HE WHISPERED.

WITH A FINAL LEAP, KAI LANDED SAFELY ON THE OTHER SIDE.
"I DID IT!" HE CHEERED, DUSTING OFF HIS HANDS.

THE PATH GREW STEEPER AND ROCKY.
KAI CLIMBED CAREFULLY, USING HIS ROPE TO PULL HIMSELF UP.

AT THE TOP OF THE HILL, KAI SPOTTED A GOLDEN GLOW.
"THE GOLDEN CHERRY BLOSSOM!" HE GASPED.

BUT AS KAI RAN TOWARD IT, A GRUMPY FOX BLOCKED HIS PATH.
"THIS IS MY HILL! GO AWAY!" THE FOX GROWLED.

KAI BOWED POLITELY. "I DON'T WANT TO FIGHT. I ONLY NEED THE GOLDEN CHERRY BLOSSOM. PLEASE LET ME PASS."

THE FOX SNARLED. "YOU'LL HAVE TO PROVE YOURSELF FIRST! SOLVE MY RIDDLE."
KAI NODDED. "I'M READY."

THE FOX ASKED, "WHAT HAS ROOTS BUT NEVER GROWS, A TOP BUT NO BODY?"
KAI THOUGHT HARD

A MOUNTAIN!" KAI FINALLY SAID.
THE FOX SMILED. "YOU'RE CLEVER. GO AHEAD, YOUNG NINJA.

KAI WALKED CAREFULLY TO THE GOLDEN CHERRY BLOSSOM.
IT GLOWED BRIGHTER AS HE APPROACHED

WHEN KAI PICKED THE BLOSSOM, A SOFT VOICE WHISPERED, "BE KIND, ALWAYS. IT MAKES YOU STRONG."
KAI NODDED. "I'LL REMEMBER.

KAI FINALLY REACHED THE VILLAGE.
SENSEI MEI GREETED HIM. "DID YOU SUCCEED?"

KAI HELD OUT THE GOLDEN CHERRY BLOSSOM.
"YES, BUT I ALSO HELPED OTHERS ALONG THE WAY," HE SAID.

SENSEI MEI SMILED PROUDLY. "YOU'VE LEARNED THE TRUE MEANING OF BEING A NINJA. WELL DONE, KAI.

THE OTHER STUDENTS CHEERED FOR KAI.
"YOU'RE A REAL NINJA NOW!" SAID HIS BEST FRIEND, LINA.

KAI PLACED THE BLOSSOM IN THE VILLAGE SHRINE.
IT SPARKLED BRIGHTLY, FILLING EVERYONE'S HEARTS WITH JOY.

THAT NIGHT, KAI LOOKED AT THE STARS.
"BEING A NINJA ISN'T JUST ABOUT MISSIONS. IT'S ABOUT HELPING OTHERS," HE THOUGHT.

FROM THAT DAY ON, KAI TRAINED EVEN HARDER.
HE WAS READY FOR ANY MISSION THAT CAME HIS WAY.

AND IN THE QUIET VILLAGE, EVERYONE KNEW KAI AS THE BRAVEST LITTLE NINJA.

KAI SMILED.

"MY JOURNEY IS JUST BEGINNING."